Detachment

Detachment
Christian
Carla R. Mancari

Celestial Literary Group

Detachment: Christian
Copyright 2018 Carla R. Mancari. All rights reserved. No part of this book may be reproduced or retransmitted in any form or by any means without the author's written permission—revised 11/6/2020.

The contents of this book are not meant to take the place of qualified medical professionals or therapists. There is no expressed or implied guarantee as to the effects of the suggestions given or liability taken.

Contents

Acknowledgments
Introduction

1. Attachments 10
Misuse of Energy

2. Conditioning 15
Cause

3. Detachments 20
Freedom

4. Detachment 1 24
Pure Awareness

5. Detachment 2 28
Finer States of Christ Consciousness

6. Detachment 3 31
From the Christ Consciousness

7. Detachments 38
Adjusting

8. Realizations 42
Awakening

9. Expansive Awareness and 47
The Void, *Indescribable*

10. Why Learn to Meditate? 64
Realize Your Spirituality

11. The Spiritual Heart Center 69
An Invitation

12. The Christ Centered Prayer ... 81
Revelation

13. The Practice 92
Three Easy Steps

14. Obstacles 104
Stepping Stones

15. Mini-Meditations 118
Staying Grounded

Summary 136

Author 139

Author's Books 142

Notes 154

Acknowledgments

Heartfelt thanks to Mary Carpenter, who reviewed and edited the manuscript. Her dedication and patience are appreciated.

A big thanks to Irene Landers for her artistic, humorous sketches. Her visual expressions are invaluable. She is always willing to help.

I am grateful to Jesus Christ for The Christ Centered Prayer Meditation revelation gift with the most profound love.

Introduction

Detachment: Christian gives an understanding of the role attachments plays in your life. It tracks detachments from the lowest state of consciousness to the Christ Consciousness's finest energy vibratory state *and* beyond. Reviewed are the Spiritual Heart Center, The Christ Centered Prayer meditation, and its practice. Also listed for your inner journey's progress, Mini-Meditations are offered.

From its conception, the Christ Centered Prayer meditation has helped individuals from all walks of life. The Christ Centered Prayer meditation offers a means of quickly and easily accessing your Spiritual Heart Center. It may enable you to become aware of the detachments. The Christ Centered Prayer is a Christian practice available for you who wish to learn to meditate and travel a direct path to your Spiritual Heart Center – your "other heart." It is here that mystical mysteries are resolved and where knowledge, understanding, insights, and wisdom reside.

Scripture verses are from The Holy Bible, King James Version, London: Syndics of Cambridge University Press, Bentley House, American Branch, New York, printed in Great Britain.

1

Attachments
Misuse of Energy

To better understand detachment, a basic understanding of attachment is necessary. Attachment is what causes suffering, binds you to this world, and limits your freedom of being. The moment you think *I, me, my,* and *mine,* attachment arises causing suffering. Attachment of any kind is the unnecessary misuse of energy. Attachment is not a realization.

The belief that you exist as a separate person allows attachment to come into existence. Thoughts rise constantly. They are vibrating energy rising as thinking, no more, no less. Thoughts in and of themselves have no emotions attached to them. You attach the conditioned descriptive judgment of good, bad, pleasurable, or painful. You do it according to your conditioned memory experiences. You give the attached emotions the power to please or to hurt you.

The attachment to pleasure can be a subtle pull in its direction. Interestingly, there are seldom, if ever, any complaints about the emotions that give pleasure; however, the rising energy is the same as for pain. One thought is no different from another. Vibrating energy is vibrating energy. Thoughts take the form and conditions that you create for them. In reality, there are never any differences and never any opposites

The moment you think "I, Me, My, Mine," attachment rises, and the attachment causes suffering. It is the personal conditioning of "I, Me, My, Mine" that creates a personal sense of a separate self. You are never separate. You are an individual expression of consciousness one with your God. "For in him we live, and move, and have our being; as certain also of your own poets have said, For we are also his offspring" (Acts 17:28).

To be attached to a separate false sense of a personal self is to suffer. You experience a lonely separate existence. You are always seeking another to fulfill your every need and happiness. It is an imaginary sense of your reality. You are a spiritually aware being. It is the false belief in a personal sense that causes an unreal experience of an imaginary false sense of self in consciousness. As you live out from this personal sense of self, you take everything personally. You are defensive, over-sensitive, and seldom listen to what is being said or seen. You want to please everyone and continue to seek approval. It is not possible.

The false concept of a personal self, who does not exist, keeps you on the edge of a life perpetuating the false concept. As a false concept of a personal self, you believe you must protect it at all times, at all cost. As memory thoughts rise, and you attach painful emotions to them, suffering occurs. It saps your energy and weakens your strength.

Thoughts are continually rising; you must decide how best they may serve you. Attaching different emotions, hate, anger, joy, or love to the rising thoughts that rise one moment and fall the next, is to attach falsely to that which cannot be sustained. Giving up the attachments to emotions (not the emotions themselves) gives you the freedom to love unconditionally.

2

CONDITIONING
The Cause

What is there that influences the way we think, speak, and act? What is the cause of attachment and the necessity for detachments? Conditioning! Conditioning is the cause of our thoughts, words, and actions. Conditioning is accomplished with labels, names, and identities given to persons, objects, feelings, thoughts, and emotions through repetition. As a conscious being, you have a mind, thoughts, and senses — hearing, taste, touch, sight, and smell — which have a natural power to receive impressions through the body organs. The thoughts and impressions are stamped with the conditioning of the culture or society you live in.

You are conditioned in thought, word, and deed from the moment you enter this world of opposites. Conditioning is continually being done by parents, friends, peers, authority figures, and politicians. According to traditional culture, religion, and political parties, your moral judgment is based on the conditioning of what is considered right or wrong, good or bad.

Because shapes and forms of objects are constructed for use, you are conditioned to think of and see their practical use, rather than know their essence. For example, a woodblock cut from a tree, then carved into a chair or table, is always seen and thought of as a chair or table. However, it remains the wood (tree/seed), and if it were burned, it would be ashes. The chair or table is only a functional concept of its reality.

When using conscious sight and thought, you see and think "chair," "table." You are not aware of purely seeing. You see a concept; thus, you do not realize pure awareness. If you are not in a state of pure awareness, your belief is in the conditioned sense-impressions.

Conditioning creates useful functional labeled concepts (such as a chair or table) to communicate and identify objects and individual beings. It also may create false concepts of thought patterns and sense-impressions. False concepts are created when you accept the appearance of anything (or anyone) as its reality. Conditioning may create a false sense of a self, separate and apart from your being's spirituality.

Let's take it a step further. Ultimately, it is about the conditioning of consciousness. From the time you are born, your conscious mind and the physical body are given a name. Repeatedly hearing your mind and body addressed with the given name causes you to identify with it as who you are. You are taught the use of I, me, my, and mine, which become personal attachments to the name. All are concepts; none is the reality of who you are. The entire package of conditioned mind, thoughts, and physical body are sense-impressions that lead you to falsely identify as a separate personal being, which you are not.

3

Detachments
Freedom

Now that you have a better understanding of attachment (chapter 1), you may come to understand detachments and their need. There are three different detachments. There isn't any relationship between the three, and one does not exist within the other. Any of the detachments do not mean indifference to persons, places, or things. As long as you are on this plane of opposites, you continue to nurture relationships and use the things of this world.

Detachments:

1. The Pure Awareness Detachment

The detachment from the physical/emotional sense of being a you/witness and freedom from attachments, which cause suffering, to the things of this earthly world.

2. Detachment from the individual finer states of the Christ

This detachment is different from the physical *pure awareness* detachment realization. It is a realization beyond the physical condition. Thus, the freedom from suffering is from a you/witness at the higher finer vibration states of consciousness, not the mind and physical states of consciousness.

3. Detachment from the Christ Consciousness may occur while realizing the Christ Consciousness' *finest* vibratory state. Once the state of Christ Consciousness *is* realized and fades, the Expansive Awareness of be-ing exists. No observer is required for this detachment realization because there is no observer as be-ing the Christ Consciousness.

~~

Detachments are the freedom from the bondage of suffering and heavy burdens. It is to take the easy yoke and find rest. For the things of this world are weighty, and you may have grown weary in the pursuit of them. "*Come unto me, all ye that labor and are heavy laden, and I will give you rest*" (Matt. 11:28).

4

Detachment - 1
Pure Awareness Detachment Realization

The Pure Awareness Detachment Realization

There are many mind states within the personal, emotional, and physical states of consciousness. All *personal* attachments to these states must be detached to realize the Pure Awareness detachment. The Pure Awareness detachment realization gives freedom from personal attachments allowing relationships and using the things in this world to be enjoyed without suffering.

Detachments are occurring during a Christ Centered Prayer practice every time a thought, image, or emotion arises and you, the witness, do not dialogue or engage. As you are merely a witness, the detachments are gradually occurring as the witness falls away. It is *subtle*, and the final Pure Awareness detachment realization occurs when you, as the "I"/witness, drops away.

What remains is Pure Awareness of the rising and falling vibrating energy. There are no labels, there is no conditioning, and there is no "I, *you.*" *Pure* is the vibrating energy rising and falling in conscious awareness. Thus, the detachment that has occurred is from the person/witness.

Your personal thinking *I, me, my,* and *mine* may not be immediately possible. It may feel strange not having any sense of self to cling to for a while. Be patient; this usually will not last long. When it does happen, it is best to stay quiet and muse with it for a while. No immediate physical activity should be resumed. Time to readjust to your surrounding environment may be necessary after any of the detachments. Understanding that God is One, and there is no other, may mean the total unraveling and elimination of the attachment to and identification with the created order. When the creation is conceived of as permanent and when bodies are perceived as all there is, power, position, and privilege are thought of as all-important.

Realizing the detachment from a person/witness can be both devastating and radiantly uplifting. The value of a free, non-suffering, non-attached life *gradually* unfolds. *"He that findeth his life shall lose it: and he that loseth his life for my sake shall find it"* (Matt. 10:39).

5

Detachment - 2
From Finer States of Christ Consciousness

Detachment Realization from The Finer Vibrations of the States of The Father/Christ Consciousness

Yes, there may be attachments within your finer states of the Father/Christ Consciousness. These attachments must also be let go of until the **_Christ Consciousness's finest vibration state_** is realized. This is true freedom. Then you may express these states without suffering. Nothing is given up except the attachment.

All states rise within Father/Christ Consciousness. As an "I/you" rises within your finer states of the Father/Christ Consciousness, a Buddha, Jesus, saint, loved one, or an object may appear. This detachment realization from the witness state is different from the *Pure Awareness* detachment realization. It is a realization beyond mind/body conditions. Thus, the freedom from suffering is at the higher, finer witness states of the Father/Christ Consciousness.

The Christ Centered Prayer practice facilitates detachment from the witness of finer states of Father/Christ Consciousness. Each time an image or object arises and the witness (you) does not dialogue or engage; detachment may occur until the finest state of the Father/Christ Consciousness is realized. With this detachment, a sense of the witness, a "you, I," ceases. There is only *be-ing* the finest State of the Father/Christ Consciousness vibration.

6

Detachment - 3
From the Christ Consciousness

Detachment realization from the *finest* state of the Father/Christ Consciousness

The detachment realization from the *finest* state of the Father/Christ Consciousness may occur once the *finest* vibration of the Father/Christ Consciousness *is* realized, *and it* fades. The expansive awareness of be-ing exists (chapter 9). No witness is required for this detachment realization to occur because there is no witness while be-ing the *finest* vibration state of the Father/Christ Consciousness.

While Expansive Awareness *is be-ing,* the *finest* Father/Christ Consciousness' state ascends without a witness. The Christ Consciousness' individual states then rise and descend. The detachment realization of the *finest* Father/Christ Consciousness vibration is possible when there are readiness and preparedness.

~~

Reverend Sandy's (a priest and retreat guide) plans did not always work out according to her expectations. She had to readjust her thinking and obey when she came for a retreat/vacation visit with me in Florida. The results of the detachment from the *finest* Christ Consciousness vibration, for her, was life-changing.

I spent two weeks in Florida with my teacher as part of a retreat/vacation. The first week I wanted to rest, pray, and reflect. The second week I wanted to spend some time at the ocean. My teacher had other plans for me.

While practicing the Christ Centered Prayer and resting in awareness with my teacher, it was unexpected, without precedence, profound, clear, and unmistakable. The Father/Christ Consciousness finest vibration detachment realization came in utter simplicity. While this realization was going on, there was no personal sense at all. The Father/Christ Consciousness finest state faded, and there was only being Expansive Awareness.

To be detached, for me, did not mean that I was indifferent or aloof. Still, I found myself strangely aware of the rising thoughts, emotions, sensations, and various streams of consciousness that rose and fell at any given moment in the day without an "I" attached. I realized that I had the power to attach or not to emotions, either positive or negative, to rising thoughts.

I neither felt like I was a saint nor a sinner. I didn't feel victorious or a failure. I just looked and decided whether to bite on a juicy rising thought with its commentary and characters.

~~

The starting point for any of the detachment realizations is awareness of the Spiritual Heart Center *area*. The Christ Centered Prayer practice is a gentle practice that may allow any of the three detachment realizations to occur. However, when realized, they may be startling, as Reverend Sandy discovered.

At first, any of the detachments may be experienced as a sense of loss. It *is* the ultimate loss: dying to the false self, the illusionary sense of a separate personal life. It may be disorienting and take time for a personal sense of self to rise again.

Yes, living out from your God source requires a reorientation in thought patterns. It requires patience and understanding *and* a sense of humor. Living in a calm state of being is not numbness. It is living as an aware, conscious being. Relinquishing all attachments to all states of consciousness, including the Father/Christ Consciousness, allows you the freedom to express unconditional love.

Jesus was aware of His God-reality. Jesus guides you through the awareness of the many realizations. The Christ Centered Prayer practice assists *you* in following Jesus.

You are so precious that Jesus was willing to lay down His life so that you may pick yours up. Embrace the spiritual nature with which you were created. Jesus' teachings, parables, and promises are recorded in the scriptures so that they may lead you to the realization of your divine origin.

If you have never tasted chocolate ice cream, can you realize what it tastes like from talking about its qualities? If you want the taste of it, what must you do? You must taste it for yourself. The same is true of the detachment realizations. Telling you about them is not the same as realizing them for yourself.

7

Detachments
Adjusting

The starting point for any detachment is awareness of the Spiritual Heart Center area (chapter 11). The Christ Centered Prayer practice (chapter 13) is a gentle practice that may allow the detachments to occur effortlessly. However, any detachment may be startling. At first, a detachment may be experienced as a sense of loss. It is the ultimate loss: dying to the false self, the illusionary sense of a separate personal life. It may be disorienting and take time for a personal sense of self to rise again.

It may feel strange not having any sense of self to cling to for a while. Be patient; this usually will not last long. When it does happen, it is best to stay quiet and muse with it for a while. No immediate physical activity should be taken.

Time to readjust to your surrounding environment may be necessary after any detachment. There is the understanding that with detachment, there is the total unraveling and elimination of the attachment to and identification with the created order. When creation is conceived as permanent, when bodies are perceived as all there is, power, position, and privilege are thought of as all-important.

You may find yourself in a conflicted emotional state when any of the detachments may occur. A detachment may challenge old loyalties and clash between the old and the new. It may have a way of changing your interest.

A detachment realization may cause your present and plans to appear distant, and the familiar less recognizable. The change may cause a direct conflict with your existing relationships, job position, or activities. The conflict of interest is at its highest intensity when you harbor an insistence on holding on to the familiar while the new overshadows it. The conflict of interest dissolves when you can let go of the familiar, making space for the current new interest that has been born of any or all of the detachments.

Yes, living out from your God source requires a reorientation in thought patterns. It requires patience and understand*ing and* a sense of humor. Living in a calm state of being is not numbness. It is living as an aware, conscious being. Relinquishing all attachments to all states of consciousness, including the Father/Christ Consciousness, allows you the freedom from the earth plane of opposites and the freedom to express unconditional love.

8

Realizations
Awakening

Realization or enlightenment is a common word used on a spiritual journey. In your spirituality, there is never any "you" to realize anything. As you have detachments and revelations, truth may be revealed.

Realizations are your nature. They confirm that eternal life is not a destination or a place. Eternal life cannot be housed or destroyed. Here and now is as good a time as any to realize eternal life. *"And this is life eternal, that they might know thee the only true God, and Jesus Christ, whom thou hast sent"* (John 17:3).

It is not necessary to remember or recall a realized truth because *you are it.* Being a realized truth, in the present, does not require memory. There is no need to remember that which you are in the present. A realization is not an experience or a past insight. A realization is a present. Memory requires a past. A realization of the truth enables you to recognize temptations for what they are and overcome them.

You are aware that your strength is of the Lord God. You may find you are no longer easily caught up in the chatter of this world. *"Let my mouth be filled with thy praise and with thy honour all the day"* (Ps. 71:8).

Not always timed according to plan, a realization may arise when least expected. Do not be quick to think that there is only one realization. There is not one grand realization. There may be many realizations in your spirituality that constitute being a fully realized (awakened) being.

Realizations transform faith into belief. With each truth realization, truth penetrates the ignorance perpetuated by the illusionary world of your imagination. Realizations cast a light of understanding within the spirituality of your being. *"The wisdom of the prudent is to understand his way: but the folly of fools is deceit"* (Prov. 14:8).

Realizations awaken you to the full awareness of the spirituality of your being. This world of opposites exists within consciousness and only in a relative sense. *"And that, knowing the time, that now it is high time to awake out of sleep: for now is our salvation nearer than when we believed"* (Rom. 13:11).

Realizations are uniquely tailored for each individual. The Christ Centered Prayer practice may gradually fine-tune you to receive the necessary realizations. You never have a reason to compare or envy another's spiritual way. Be convinced yours is perfect for you.

9

**Expansive Awareness
and
The Void**
Indescribable

Expansive Awareness and the Void are often referred to as realizations. They are *not.* This is because there is no consciousness present to realize either of them, and they have no adequate description. All that can be done is to tell you *about* them. In Expansive Awareness, there is only an Expansive Awareness of be-ing. When you return from the Void, you only know you know.

Expansive Awareness

Beyond all states of consciousness, there is Expansive Awareness of *be-ing.* There is no transition from the highest state of the Father/Christ Consciousness to Expansive Awareness. The Christ Consciousness state fades, and *be-ing* expansive awareness remains.

There is "emptiness," "expansive-ness," and yet, there is "fullness." There is "nothing," and yet, "everything." You are a spiritual being sojourning in a physical sense form upon this earth, but the greater reality is in the infinite life of God-Expansive Awareness.

After the Father/Christ Consciousness's final state *is* realized and fades, the Expansive Awareness of be-ing exists. Being detached from the Christ Consciousness's final state does not require an observer because, as there is only the ***be-ing*** the finest vibration of the Christ Consciousness, there is no observer to observe. While Expansive Awareness *is be-ing* the Father/Christ Consciousness state again rises without an observer. The awareness of individual consciousness, mind-consciousness, and body consciousness eventually rises and falls, and a witness state returns.

There is no beginning and no end when being Expansive Awareness. For a golden moment, the reality of being is expressed in silent Expansive Awareness. The descending way recurs when consciousness rises. Within Expansive Awareness, the pre-existent "Word" spontaneously rises, and through it, all things are made. "All *things were made by him, and without him was not anything made that was made"* (John I:3).

Once awakened to the truth of "no person," there is no person to suffer or die. The "I" is a tool of communication, not identification. Recognition of truth is real freedom. *"And ye shall know the truth, and the truth shall make you free"* (John 8:32).

~~

Reverend Sandy (a priest and retreat leader) attempts to explain her existence as Expansive Awareness. She had to live with the Expansive Awareness of be-ing for over a year before she attempted to put it into words. Expansive Awareness is difficult to put into words because words are not it. Taking the time and living *It*, as Reverend Sandy did, was the wise thing to do.

~~

Working with my teacher, I moved back from the understandable yet mistaken attachment to a separate individual false sense of self (called "Sandy"). Its corresponding feelings of alienation and suffering, to being one aware, is true freedom and eternal life. That truth, for me, is awareness of oneness be-ing.

The subsequent realization of consciousness rising in awareness clarifies the long quoted "unity in diversity "Trinity," or 'three in one' so commonly referred to in our tradition as a mystery. I agree mystery is mysterious, but it is not unreal. Granted, it cannot be 'grasped' by the mind because it transcends the mind. As we know, mind, senses, reason, will, intellect, and memory all rise within conscious awareness, but they are not "Awareness."

I experienced myself moving from my usual separate personal sense of being 'Sandy' into a realization of oneness in Christ and then dissolving within through this oneness to the be-ing—expansive awareness. In a very real way, all must awaken from the identification with an individual, separate personal sense of being to the oneness of the awareness of the Christ Consciousness where Jesus Christ is one in His Father. This is to know the Father as Jesus knows the Father. Je-

sus is the way, and the way to the Father is through Him.

My teacher continued to work with me, and while being Expansive Awareness, she instructed me to allow the Christ Consciousness to rise and fall. The finest vibration rose, and the other states of consciousness were rising and falling. Becoming aware of the Christ Consciousness rising and falling seemed natural, and it was occurring without the benefit of an observer.

This is no longer a platitude for me but a direct truth. Sandy to Jesus and through Jesus to the Father/Christ Consciousness, to expansive awareness be-ing without being aware "of" anything or anyone. It is the journey home spoken of from all ages.

This truth unfolded during a silent prayer session with my teach-

er. I was aware of becoming smaller and smaller as an individual personal sense of Sandy until 'I' ultimately wholly disappeared, dissolving, gone. What remained had no object of perception, no separate personal sense, just oneness of be-ing Expansive Awareness, being without being conscious "of" anything or anyone. It has also taken over a year to begin to assimilate and articulate in words how expansive awareness has led to an understanding and wisdom, wisdom I continue to grow into.

~~

Mary, a meditation teacher, also moved from the finest Father/Christ Consciousness into Expansive Awareness. The results left her out of balance with her immediate surroundings. Mary was fortunate that her Christ Consciousness realization detachment occurred while she was attending a Christ

Centered Prayer retreat. She was in a safe, quiet environment that allowed her to adjust to the Christ Consciousness detachment realization.

Mary attempts to put into words the indescribable. The Expansive Awareness effect is profound. Mary's be-ing Expansive Awareness leaves her with a greater understanding of unconditional love. She is impressed with the harmful effects of judging.

The Father/Christ Consciousness drops away to everything-ness, nothing-ness, and all-ness to being Expansive Awareness. Then the Christ Consciousness rises, and mind and body consciousness rises, just rising and falling. No labels, no identity. I returned so detached that, for a time, I could not mentally function very well. I could not read the retreat schedule or comprehend the writing on the schedule. I could not remember if it was Thursday or Friday. I was changed. My consciousness had changed.

I moved to the Christ Consciousness. One with myself, one with Oneness, so comfortable, so whole. The Christ Consciousness fades to my be-ing Expansive Awareness.

Upon returning to my individual state of consciousness, I was aware of healing, purification, and forgiveness. I realized the power of the Spiritual Heart Center and that the purifying of energy provides more capacity to love in all things. I had an awareness that judging puts an iron gate before a loving heart.

~~

Expansive Awareness is beyond the finest vibratory state of the

Father/Christ Consciousness. There is no *I*, no person. The *I,* or person, has no reality, so why create one? *"Thou shalt not make unto thee any graven image or any likeness of anything that is in heaven above, or that is in the earth beneath, or that is in the water under the earth"* (Ex. 20:4).

THE VOID

The void is not void-less. It is the Almighty indescribable God from which all proceeds. You can only be amazed at the wonder of It. *"He stretcheth out the north over the empty place, and hangeth the earth upon nothing"* (Job 26:7).

You may be surprised and confused that there is this Void God. Your first inclination is to describe *It*, not possible. You struggle to understand *It*; you cannot. You struggle to talk about *It*; you cannot.

As you return from the Void, you know that you know the unknown, the Almighty Void God none can describe. Once known, you know it will be for others to venture within, to know they know for themselves. You are left with the knowledge there are two types of individuals: the one who knows the Void God and *cannot* describe it and the one who does not know the Void God and can describe it.

The Almighty Void God is truly all in all and beyond all description. The Supreme Being is beyond words, thoughts, consciousness, and awareness. Whatever you can imagine *It* is, it is not. Whatever you say, *It* is, it is not.

~~

Reverend Sandy always wanted a definition of the Void. She

would try in many ways to trick my giving her one; it never worked. When she found out for herself, the tricks were over.

Oh, Oh, Oh, how long I waited for the Void and the no-thing-ness. This is a strange, strange journey full of twists and turns. How many times I wondered what "pure transcendence" would be like, and now I am told by my teacher not to get carried away with it to the point of desiring to go off into the Void.

I was not trying to let go and go there; I just went there. I was on a nine-day private intensive retreat with a rigorous schedule of silent prayer and solitude. I was simply practicing the silent Christ Centered Prayer, as my teacher had instructed. As thoughts, emotions, and sensations rose, I only again became aware of my spiritual heart center area, nothing more, nothing less. I returned and rested in awareness.

After three days of intense silence, I was just sitting there, and without warning, without fanfare, without doing anything, it just happened. I just slipped from awareness into the Void, and the next thing I knew, I was coming up from a deep place, not knowing how I got there, how long I'd been there, or even remembering wanting to go there. Yes, the Void is indescribable.

The Void indeed made an impact on my life. Coming off the retreat, I noticed people were strangely beautiful. I found myself perceiving goodness in people in whom I previously saw nothing to commend. Now they seemed full of potential.

Perhaps it was merely that my potential was expanding. I was amazed at myself. The sharp edge was not there. I was relating more kindly, and the world seemed to be relating to me more kindly.

Returning to a householder and priest's hectic demands, I carried with me a sense of awe and gratitude. Nothing had changed, but everything had changed. It would take years for the event to be integrated and to settle.

It has taken years for me to put pen to paper about this retreat. I speak of it now simply to say the Void exists. In retrospect, I am now aware that Its value is not in "Itself" an end, but rather, one means in more fully understanding and appreciating in this life some of the mystery of God. This mystery to be lived fully in each individual life as compassion, mercy, peace, justice, and unconditional love.

Reverend Sandy now understood why the Void was indescribable. She, too, could not put it into words. She finally settled for "knowing she knew."

~~

Saying how either Expansive Awareness or the Void may affect an individual can be difficult. Some are in a daze, and some are left dumbfounded for a time. Others have reported frustration with the inability to describe them. No matter the effects, Expansive Awareness or the Void is what it is, and It remains the Expansive Awareness and the Almighty God Void that truth-seekers must venture forth to know for themselves.

This entire chapter is *about* Expansive Awareness and the Void God, but not one word describes them. Expansive Awareness and the Void simply are. *"And this is life eternal, that they might know thee the only true God, and Jesus Christ, whom thou hast sent"* (John 17:3).

10

**Why
Learn To Meditate?**
Realize Your Spirituality

Why learn to meditate? A silent meditation practice may softly guide you to access your Spiritual Heart Center (chapter 11). The ultimate work of meditation practice is that you may realize your spirituality.

Meditation may transform your life into a more balanced and contented life. This may only occur when you are an aware, conscious individual expression manifesting from your consciousness's spirituality state. Intellectually you may know something is missing in your life. You may want to believe that your spirituality is realized in philosophical teachings from which you may achieve a temporary emotional high. Yes, but an emotional high is a temporary fix.

It's easy to get lost in a world that gives you a high one day and a low the next. Worldly wisdom or intellectual pursuits may temporarily satisfy, but they leave you without your spirituality's aware presence. That is what is missing.

To intentionally or unintentionally seek the different metaphysical teachings to realize what is missing may stimulate your mind and cause you to feel uplifted. You would continuously be rising to the mental state of consciousness, and the mind tends to keep you where it feels good. Your seeking to reach your detached state of consciousness based on outer pursuits is like the miner easily attracted to fool's gold. You may become content to fulfill your quest by only seeking what glitters. It may be shiny and may look like the real thing, but the real thing it is not.

There is nowhere out here that you can realize what is missing. It's the mind's work to want to take you on an outer journey. That is what the mind does best. Silent Meditation takes you on an inner journey to what may be missing. It is all about an inner journey, a journey that begins not out here but within you.

Why learn to meditate? Meditation practice is a vehicle that delivers you to your destination. Meditation practice may endow you with a greater awareness of an inner path that acknowledges your spirituality. You may connect with your root being. You may discover that you are more than a name. You are more than an individual who walks this earth. Yours is more than the physical sense of the life of which you are so attached. Yours is a spiritual nature.

Perhaps you have a strong opposition to a constant reminder that you have a greater reality. But you can't separate yourself from that which you are. Learn to meditate and awaken to the good news that there is more.

Meditation guides your footsteps directly to the silence of awareness of your Spiritual Heart Center (chapter 11). You have the necessary wherewithal to accomplish any necessary detachment. You live at a time and in a world where many choices are presented. Meditation is one of them.

Why not take a direct inner path? Why not say yes to a meditation that requires no outer intermediary. When you consent and awaken to the spirituality of your inner source, the unreal may recede. Your spirituality may continuously be revealed in the heart-packed action within your Spiritual Heart Center.

11

The Spiritual Heart Center
An Invitation

An old story goes something like this: After God had created humankind, God called one of the angels and asked the angel to hide the one thing God wished to conceal.

"I have finished except for one thing: the mystery of life. Where shall you hide it?" God asked the angel.

"I will hide it in outer space," responded the excited angel.

"No," God said, *"one day, someone will easily find it there."*

"All right, I will hide it on the moon. Surely it will not be found there?"

"No, no," said God, *"one day, they will be able to look there also. Hmmm, I have it! Let's put it within them. They would never think to look there!"*

~~

There is a gentle, subtle vibrating center within you (in the center of the chest, between the breasts). It's called the Spiritual Heart Center because of the proximity of the physical heart. This energetic, vibrating center is also referred to as your "other heart." The Spiritual Heart Center is well known in the East as the Fourth Chakra, Anahata Chakra.

Although often written about and discussed, the Spiritual Heart Center's direct availability and easy access are *often* ignored. It is the most neglected entrance into the inner sanctuary of your being. There are seven spiritual centers (chakras) within the physical body. They begin at the base of the spine and end at the top of the head. These vibrating energy centers are located three below the Spiritual Heart Center and three above it. The Spiritual Heart Center is the powerhouse that influences the centers above and below it.

This pure vibrating energy center does not have a particular religious affiliation. Members from any religion, or none, may access it. The Spiritual Heart Center is the connection to all states and levels of consciousness. And depending on the state of consciousness, which you choose to realize Buddha, Hindu, Christ, or any other, that is the one you may realize. It is amazing!

It is here beyond all religions that mystical mysteries are resolved, where knowledge, understanding, insights, and wisdom reside. It is here that your spirituality is realized. Most importantly, with meditation's help, resolutions are born in moments of critical situations, and the answers needed in your practical life may come forth.

Though this powerful energy center is as close to you as your physical heart, it may seem strange and unfamiliar; you may shy away from this important center from fear of the unknown. It may require courage for you to venture beyond the known into the depths of your Spiritual Heart Center. You may prefer to stick with what you believe you know.

Fortunately, meditation gently guides you to the point where you may access your Spiritual Heart Center. This is your birthright and may be reflected in your daily living. For many, the heart is a symbol of love, and so it should be, as it contains the love of you and all individuals. Meditation continuously connects you with your Spiritual Heart Center in the Oneness of love. The unconditional love of your Spiritual Heart Center may guide you through your daily activities.

Every individual, every creature, is a loving expression of the Oneness of unconditional love. The one who tills the soil, the one who plants the seed, the one who encourages the growth, the one who gathers the crops, the one who packages it, ships it, stocks it, and the one who brings the banquet to the table for your nourishment: all are expressions of the unconditional love that nurtures the universe. You cannot eat a meal without recognizing that the least upon the table is an expression of that unconditional love.

During a meditation practice, in the awareness of your Spiritual Heart Center, you may realize an unconditional love that has a natural ability to include, embrace, and permeate all individual beings. It gives all to all and holds back nothing from those who are aware and receptive. When you rest in the silent awareness of your Spiritual Heart Center, you possess the natural inclination to share this kind of love. In sharing it, you come into the aware and receptive awareness of *your* unconditional loving nature. It is a nature that knows it is in the giving back that is the foundation of a contented, full life.

Look in the least expected place: within you. There you will bask in the silent awareness of your Spiritual Heart Center, your "other heart." The Spiritual Heart Center invites and beckons you now to go within so that you may realize what is yours. It does not matter how isolated you may have felt in the past; the radiant light of your Spiritual Heart Center will hold you in unconditional love.

All the strength and action you could ever desire in your life exist in every vibration of your Spiritual Heart Center, your "other heart." The vibrating energy is an invulnerable power that may dissipate sorrowful remorse, soothe a troubled heart, and restore relationships. The Spiritual Heart Center may guide your footsteps into an awareness of your inherent spirituality. Here you may become aware of your uniqueness as an individual expression of consciousness. You may become aware of this power as you practice meditation.

This power radiates a light that you may step into and with which you may be as One as you rest in the silent awareness of your Spiritual Heart Center *area*. Your spiritual power is a center of compassion, clarity, discernment, and wisdom. You may become aware that, indeed, less of this world is more, and more of this world is not necessary. The power to wash away greed and bathe you in unconditional love resides in your Spiritual Heart Center. The power of love is without limits, and it cannot be diminished. It is a protective strength and eternal grace that accompanies you always on your life's journey, and it envelops your conscious mind.

You may have been led to believe that the conscious mind is the power to be harnessed. Yes, the mind is a powerful instrument, and when it is focused on the things of this world, it may perform seemingly magical feats and fulfill desires. But the mind, in and of itself, has no power. All it can do is what is given to it from within.

The mind may manifest desired attractions, but it may also cause mischief and create obstacles where there are none. To work only with the mind is to deny yourself the opportunity to go beyond the mind to where the power exists: your Spiritual Heart Center. The power is given directly to you from within. You decide whether to invest the power in the manifestations of attractions in this world. You may use or misuse your power of vibrating energy.

If you choose to build your life with a thought-focused mind, you are building on quicksand. Attractions created by thoughts follow the path of thoughts: they rise, they fall. The mind left to its own devices is easily distracted. A thought-focused mind is an attempt to realize your spirituality by force, which is not possible! The peace, joy, and comfort you seek exist not within the mind but within your Spiritual Heart Center.

With meditation practice, you may realize the power within and hear the silence. You will recognize that awareness of your Spiritual Heart Center is readily available to you within this silence. From here, whatever is necessary to meet your needs manifests without relying on the mind's creations.

Become aware of the power within your Spiritual Heart Center. This essential power dissolves the darkness created by ignorance and the fear that darkness breeds. Discover a quiet that is only attainable when you regularly connect with the power of your Spiritual Heart Center.

No code, no secret password, no referral, no formal introduction is needed for you to meet and access your Spiritual Heart Center. It will never be enough for you just to know about your Spiritual Heart Center. You will always long to connect to and access it. *The Christ Centered Prayer Meditation* is the boat that will carry you across the river into your Spiritual Heart Center. Get in and take the ride of your life, which will take you to a new beginning of you.

12

The
Christ Centered
Prayer Method
Revelation

How confused are you? Do the many different contemplations, meditations, and concentration practices have you confused? Is there a method that can help you to become a more aware, conscious individual?

Is there a meditation method that may allow you to realize the detachment realizations? A method without all of the time and energy consumption required? Yes, there is. It's the Christ Centered Prayer Meditation.

The Christ Centered Prayer Method is a silent contemplative prayer practice revealed by Jesus Christ who insisted, "Teach them the Christ Centered Prayer and be assured; this generation is ready to receive it." The Christ Centered Prayer Method is offered as a means to easily access your Spiritual Heart Center so that you may establish, through the power of the Holy Spirit, your relationship with the risen Lord. It is a simple method to learn. It acknowledges and builds upon all previous contemplative teaching, tradition, and biblical reference.

What makes the Christ Centered Prayer Method the pearl of great price, the Holy Grail of silent prayer methods? It is a revelation - the strait gate and narrow way to the Holy Spirit in the name of Jesus Christ. The Christ Centered Prayer Method is a unique contribution to the inner journey of detachments. It is the direct path to your inner life with Jesus Christ and beyond.

The Christ Centered Prayer Method encompasses all of the various realizations that inform and may prepare you for an awareness state of consciousness. It is all about an inner journey to the realized awakened state of being. The Christ Centered Prayer Method's simplicity is both its difficulty and its strength. Its most significant difficulty is that it is an easy practice. There are no complicated instructions with rigid rules and demanding postures. Because individuals may be accustomed to prayer methods that require a measure of difficulty, it easily becomes difficult. To be so easy and yet so profound in its ability to reveal detachments is also its strength. It can only leave you in awe!

The Christ Centered Prayer Method supports a journey well worth taking. Any journey worth taking is worth the loving patience required. Jesus is patient with you at all times, through all of your ups and downs. Now it is your turn to be patient and trust the Christ of your being knows precisely where you are, what you need, and moves you along accordingly. *"But he knoweth the way that I take: when he hath tried me, I shall come forth as gold"* (Job 23:10).

All silent prayers have their value, but there are differences. The Christ Centered Prayer Method cuts to the chase. It allows nothing to stand between you and the reality of your God being through the power of the Holy Spirit, in the name of Jesus Christ. You may be firmly established in truth. Rooted and grounded in love, your silent prayer method and your life are built upon hallowed ground. *"That Christ may dwell in your hearts by faith; that ye, being rooted and grounded in love, May be able to comprehend with all saints what is the breadth, and length, and height; And to know the love of Christ, which passeth knowledge, that ye might be filled with all the fulness of God" (Ephesians 3:17-19).*

The Christ Centered Prayer Method is graced with infinite power and profound rest. It is a subtle, calm inner Christian prayer method that allows you to move effortlessly into pure awareness. Here you may identify with your God source.

The Christ Centered Prayer Method is not in competition with other silent contemplative prayer methods. There is the delightful and relative ease with the Christ Centered Prayer Method. It drops familiar traditional aids such as a sacred word, thought, image, sound, or breath as it articulates a simplification of the ancient traditions.

The receiving, cultivating, and maintaining of Jesus' gift of "peace that passes understanding" is foundational to Christian discipleship. This Christian contemplative prayer method facilitates a posture of alert receptivity and cultivates a profound silence. It becomes inner peace. Within this peace, you may awaken to the attachments that would hold you to the many attractions of this world of appearances.

Learning to meditate and making a change from your routine can be challenging. You have been conditioned "to do" and sometimes "overdo" to get what you want. You push, shove, and drive yourself to the brink to get what you believe you want. It is always getting and holding on. Effort, effort, all is an effort.

Now you are instructed to do the opposite of what you have been taught: no pushing, no shoving, no holding on, and no driving yourself anywhere. The most significant effort is to show up and be patient. Your inner journey is unique to you.

You may go beyond the mind-body state of consciousness. Going beyond the mind may seem absurd, challenging, and undesirable. You may want to stay with the mind-body consciousness. The mind takes you on an outer journey. Its destination is governed by the attraction of appearances and false concepts. A prayerful meditation practice takes you on an inner journey to the aware spirituality of your being.

Jesus went beyond the traditions and the teachings of His day. Jesus revealed through His example and teaching that you, too, can go beyond the traditions of your day. Jesus never condemned traditional teachings. He fulfilled the law while revealing life eternal. His was a kingdom not of this world. The Christ Centered Prayer Method may slowly, carefully, and lovingly restore the remembrance of that kingdom.

The God that is known by faith dwells within you always. The

Christ-Centered prayer method is for you interested in responding to God without mental or verbal words, in solitude, simplicity, and silence. Jesus guides you through His Holy Spirit to your spirituality. *"Jesus saith unto him, I am the way, the truth, and the life: no man cometh unto the Father, but by me"* (John 14:6).

The Christ Centered Prayer Method may guide where truth, hidden for all ages, is revealed. It points you beyond words and images. Once the method's value is appreciated, there is joy in a practice that may gift your life with an aware presence of Jesus.

This world fears what it does not understand or cannot destroy. This world believed it could destroy and put to death the salvation and freedom teaching of Jesus. It could not. It did not. The pure awareness of your being is just be-ing without definition — nothing more, nothing less. *"And God said unto Moses, I AM that I AM: . . ."* (Exodus 3:14).

You tend to attach and identify with what has been created and conditioned (a false self). Become aware that you are creation "itself," the spirituality from which all is manifested. In coming home to the spirituality of your being at the deepest level, you may have the ability to remember what your life is all about.

The Christ Centered Prayer Method may keep you centered, balanced, and at peace during transitional times and times of crises. It is your shelter during the storm and your resting place during the calm. It is a resting in the awareness of the presence of the Christ of your being.

The Christ Centered Prayer Method fulfills Jesus' invitation to

"Come and find rest for your souls." With Jesus as a model, scriptures as a reference, tradition as custodian, sacraments as a celebration, and selfless service as a mission, the Christ Centered Prayer Method draws its source, sustenance, and direction. You are guided quietly and efficiently to realize all that you are and always have been.

The Christ Centered Prayer Method promises nothing, and yet, it may deliver all. It is for you to take advantage of a Christian prayer method that thoroughly and painstakingly carries you to the awakened state beyond an illusionary world. You need to know how to turn within to access your Spiritual Heart Center area. The Christ Centered Prayer practice is the "how to."

13

The Practice
Three Easy Steps

How many motivational speakers must you listen to, and how often to motivate you to start a meditation practice? Why look to others to lift your spirit and move you to realize your detachments? Your Spiritual Heart Center *is* the most incredible motivational speaker. The Christ Centered Prayer of awareness practice may ground you in constant *self-*motivation.

As a follower of Jesus Christ, you may walk a spiritual path to recognizing and accepting Jesus Christ's teaching. The Christ Centered Prayer practice carefully responds to Jesus Christ's invitation to *"come,"* and painstakingly leads you on a spiritual journey to your all-inclusive Christ presence. The practice articulates a simplification of an ancient tradition. The practice does not require a sacred word because *you are* the sacred *Word*, the "Word" that existed in the beginning. *"In the beginning was the Word, and the Word was with God, and the Word was God. The same was in the beginning with God. All things were made by him; and without him was not anything made that was made"* (John I: 1-3).

The Christ Centered Prayer meditation invites you to rest in the "Word" who you are in the awareness of your Spiritual Heart Center area (chapter 11), *"And the Word was made flesh, and dwelt among us (and we beheld his glory, the glory as of the only begotten of the Father,) full of grace and truth"* (John I: 14).

The practice is simple and easy. There is no time prescribed rituals, words, thoughts, sounds, images, or breath. The Christ Centered Prayer is an easy method of awareness practice that you can quickly learn. Sit comfortably on a couch or chair; sitting on the floor is optional. If your health does not permit you to practice in a sitting position, you may lie down if sitting is problematic. Over time, you will find that your inner practice moves in the direction of a minimum amount of effort. *A word of **CAUTION:*** Never practice any form of contemplation, quiet time, meditation, or awareness, even for a moment, while driving, operating machinery, or at any time when your safety may be at risk.

The Practice:

1. Sit comfortably, rest hands on the lap or by your sides, close your eyes, slowly, deeply inhale, and slowly exhale. Relax your entire body, and continue to breathe normally.

2. Consciously rest in the awareness of your Spiritual Heart

Center *area* (center of the chest, between the breasts).

3. When thoughts or sensations arise, do not dialogue, converse, engage, or respond, again return to rest in the awareness of your Spiritual Heart Center *area.*

~~

Is that easy enough? There is no need to complicate The Christ Centered Prayer practice. Easy *does* work. The practice takes you directly to your Spiritual Heart Center without any intermediary or mediation. However, you must do the practice.

Hearing, touching, seeing, tasting, and smelling are impressions received through perception's physical body organs. These sense impressions may draw your immediate attention. Instantly, return to your Spiritual Heart Center *area*.

Practice the silent Christ Centered Prayer at any time before a meal and at least two hours after a meal (the changing energy vibration will interfere with the digestion process). Begin the prayer for a few minutes, and allow it to extend itself naturally over time. There is no prescribed length of time required.

At the end of a prayer period, take a moment to become consciously aware of your mental and physical senses as they rise before returning to your normal activities. Remember, you are not trying to make anything happen. You are not seeking to *feel* anything. The mind feels. You are resting in awareness of your Spiritual Heart Center *area* beyond the mind and body states of consciousness.

Be consistent and practice the Christ Centered Prayer meditation twice-a-day. When sitting on a chair, you may wish to sit on one with arms for support. Sitting on a cushion on the floor and using a prayer shawl are options. If, for any reason, you find it difficult to become aware of the Spiritual Heart Center *area*, place your hand upon the Spiritual Heart Center area for the first few prayer meditations.

You may already have formed the habit of practicing a different prayer meditation. An established habit is not always easy to discontinue, especially if it is one of long-standing. A habit is an act of interest often repeated. Replacing one habitual prayer practice with another need not be difficult.

If a previous meditation prayer practice rises to compete with your new practice, do not get upset. To struggle only reinforces the old habit. With loving-kindness, allow the old established prayer practice to rise and treat it as you would any other thought. Do not dialogue. Return to rest in the awareness of your Spiritual Heart Center area. Gradually, the old practice will no longer rise.

Change of a prayer practice is a natural progression on your spiritual walk. Jesus Christ has been waiting for you. He will lovingly welcome the change. Surrender effortlessly, silently, and directly into the recognition of the fullness of your God nature.

You cannot separate yourself from the Word, which was in the beginning and was made flesh. The Word is made flesh, and it remains the Word of God. The Word of God is the eternal truth. *"Of his own will begat he us with the word of truth, that we should be a kind of first fruits of his creatures"* (James I: 18).

Without extraneous dialogue, stringent guidelines, or complicated definitions, the Christ-centered prayer meditation practice bypasses potential distractions that the mind loves to create. Be faithful, patient, and disciplined in your Christ Centered Prayer meditation practice. It is not wise or useful to judge or evaluate your practice based on your experiences.

The fruit of the prayer is always realized in daily life, as the Holy Spirit, in the name of Jesus Christ, insinuates itself spontaneously. *"But the fruit of the Spirit is love, joy, peace, longsuffering, gentleness, goodness, faith, meekness, temperance: against such there is no law"* (Galatians 5:22-23).

Your chosen path has a particular state of consciousness, be it the Buddha, Allah, Krishna, or the Christ. You should always practice your meditation prayer with those who support your chosen path's state of consciousness. Believing or insists that it does not matter will not change the spiritual principle of like consciousness's vibrations. If you insist on continuing to mix and explore, you are creating an obstacle to finding your way by the "strait gate and narrow way." *"Strive to enter in at the strait gate: for many, I say unto you, will seek to enter in, and shall not be able"* (Luke 13:24).

As you practice the Christ Centered Prayer, you may discover that the mind finds a way to distract you from becoming aware of your Spiritual Heart Center *area.* The mind is an expert at creating obstacles during a silent meditation prayer practice. Again and again, return to rest in the awareness of your Spiritual Heart Center area.

Your spoken words, as well as your thoughts, vibrate, and go forth. Be faithful to your Christ Centered Prayer practice and keep your actions gentle. Think twice before you speak, three times before you act. What you send out by the spoken word or thought will undoubtedly, "return to sender."

The surrender to Jesus Christ and the flow of your life should be seamless 24/7. There is not any time when you are other than a spiritual being. Your daily life's activities are not separate from your daily silent Christ Centered Prayer meditation practice.

Your inner guidance is seamless. You may come to be as aware of Jesus' abiding presence in your practical living as you are during your silent prayer meditation practice. Your life's daily work should not be sequestered from your prayer practice. When you open your eyes and get up from your cushion, your prayer does not end.

Practice is the key. Sit for a few minutes, twice-a-day, and rest in the awareness of your Spiritual Heart Center *area* again and again. Like the prodigal son, you are returning to your Father's house. *"I will arise and go to my father and say unto him, Father, I have sinned against heaven, and before thee"* (Luke 15:18).

Jesus Christ awaits your return. With patience, you will find the Christ Centered Prayer meditation practice has a life of its own. Relax. Enjoy, and let the prayer *do* you.

14

Obstacles
Stepping Stones

The Christ Centered Prayer practice may turn obstacles into stepping stones that lead to the blessed peace within. The following are a few of the obstacles that the mind may revel in. Your awareness of them may shorten their lifespan and shorten the path to detachments.

Obstacles:

1. Alone - Lonely

As you progress with the Christ Centered Prayer practice, you may feel a sense of discomfort and loneliness because you may think of it as being alone. There is a difference between alone and lonely. However, both have in common the inner message *one* (al*one* and l*one*ly). Alone rests in the "One." Lonely seeks the One. This world has so many tempting attractions to chase.

You may, at times, do anything not to stay home alone.

When you are attached to a separate sense of a personal self, you experience a separate existence. You experience a sense of being lonely. Loneliness seeks a more profound presence of your nature, the Oneness.

Alone and lonely are no longer obstacles once you are no longer drawn to the background noise and chatter in your home environment. When you live with the quiet, you may come closer to realizing your true nature. The inner and outer layers may merge in a calm, peaceful environment, an environment where loneliness does not exist, and being alone is restful, not restless.

2. Attention

Attention is your interest "instantly" alerted by the rising of thoughts, senses, or sense impressions (acting as stimuli) within your consciousness. The state of an object of interest, holding your attention, is called focused concentration. Attention becomes an obstacle when it attaches you to thought, emotion, or sense-impression.

Attention is the mind's most devious obstacle. It is the easiest for the mind to use during a silent prayer practice. Your attention is immediately attracted to whatever appears within your conscious mind. As your attention is attracted, it may seem to have a will of its own.

You subject yourself to suffering, pain, or pleasure by attending to or attaching emotions to the conditioned sense impressions or rising thoughts. It is your attracted interest that holds your attention. The greater the attraction, the greater chance the attention may become an obstacle.

Thoughts and sense impressions do serve a purpose on this planet when not practicing a silent prayer. They allow a conscious flexible exploration of rising thoughts and sensations that may contribute to creativity, ideas, or resolutions. As you continue the Christ Centered Prayer practice, the attention obstacle may gradually decrease. You may have a greater awareness of your spiritual nature. You have a choice over which thoughts and sensations you engage, act upon, or let go. You are in charge. This is inner freedom.

3. Complacency

You may become satisfied with your realized spiritual unfoldment. Complacency becomes an obstacle when you have lulled yourself into the false belief that you have surrendered enough. When your spiritual progress is at its smoothest, your boat may rock, and the complacency temptation will rise — understanding why your boat should be rocked during what appears as smooth sailing may be challenging.

Complacency often invites a stiff-necked resistant response to an inner or outer nudge to take another step on the straight and narrow way. The Christ Centered Prayer practice takes you beyond, into turbulent deep waters. A struggle with temptation can make you stronger, more convicted. Yours is a spiritual nature with many facets. The willingness to embrace the difficulties of yet another unknown facet of your spiritual nature allows your realized spirituality transition to be a more welcomed one.

4. Inflexibility

You may want to sit for your first practice of the day in the morning and the second during the afternoon or evening. If you find getting in a daily second practice is difficult because you cannot find the time due to work, errands, children, and a million other things on your schedule, it is understandable. Any change in your daily routine can be met with resistance.

All too often, you may be attached to a particular time or place for your practice. You want everything to be the same. This may be ideal but not always practical. An active lifestyle may require flexibility at any time. Flexibility with your Christ Centered

Prayer practice gives you the freedom to adjust to new routines.

Be flexible. Restrooms are everywhere, aren't there? You go to the bathroom sometime during your busy day, don't you? So, use one for a minute. It is that easy. A John can be accommodating. In fact, "John" may become your *best* friend.

5. Greener Pastures

You may be one who believes the grass is greener just beyond your own practice. It is difficult to remain faithful to your Christ Centered Prayer practice and progress if you have only one eye on where you are and the other on seeking greener pastures. In this world, greener pastures may appear one day and fade the next.

Where you are is where the grass is the greenest. If you are tempted to other pastures, the grass will be just as green, no greener. This is a world of many pastures. You could easily wander from one pasture to the next. The greener pasture that you seek is the one you are standing in, and with the maintenance of the Christ Centered Prayer, the greener *it* becomes. The green pastures do not change. You do. The brilliance is within you. Stay with your Christ Centered Prayer practice.

6. Internal Dialogue

In the Christ Centered Prayer practice, internal dialogue is a conditioned response to rising thoughts or sense impressions (hearing, touch, sight, taste, and smell). It is the busy work of the mind. Internal dialogue is an obstacle that produces no benefit. It sidetracks and stalls a silent prayer practice.

When your attention is attracted to rising thoughts, emotions, or senses, an internal dialogue may begin. Dialoguing is an obstacle that interferes with the immediacy of consciously returning to the awareness of your Spiritual Heart Center area. Dialoguing negates awareness of the present moment of silence, and any spiritual realizations of your God-given nature will be overshadowed and slip beneath the radar.

Internal dialogue deals primarily with memories or future expectations (planning). Neither memories of the past nor expectations of the future exist in the present. When a memory rises with an attached emotion (positive or negative), dialoguing recreates the event as if it were happening in the present. Such indulgence serves no useful purpose. Not dialoguing with rising thoughts or memories is essential.

If you do *not* dialogue with rising thoughts, emotions, sensations, and images, they will *not* become obstacles – they will fade. Not dialoguing with the rising attractions of this world, in or out of prayer practice, allows you to, *"Be still, and know that I am God: . . ."* (Ps.46:10).

7. Mixing

It is important to remember you are working with your individual expressions of consciousness, and to mix is an obstacle to your progress. A chosen way has a particular energy vibration state of consciousness, be it the Buddha, Allah, Krishna, or the Christ. You should always practice your meditation practice with an individual or individuals who support your chosen way — state of consciousness. To mix is an obstacle to your progress.

To believe or insist that it does not matter will not change the spiritual principle of like consciousness. If you insist on mixing and exploring, you create an obstacle to finding your way by the strait gate and narrow way. Your Christ Centered Prayer practice is not a social event. The Christ Centered Prayer is a sacred, silent prayer practice. Treat it as such.

~~

The Christ Centered Prayer practice establishes you in the presence of Jesus' unconditional, nonjudgmental love emanating within the Christ Consciousness — your consciousness. You do not need to get upset with any obstacle or whatever rises within your consciousness. Just renew your priority and continue your prayer practice.

As you progress on your chosen way, it is your responsibility to guard and protect each state of consciousness you have realized. The straight and narrow way is just that – straight and narrow. Creating obstacles and detours only delays the awakening to your spirituality you are seeking. *"Strive to enter in at the strait gate: for many, I say unto you, will seek to enter in, and shall not be able"* (Luke 13:24).

You are always working on yourself. It is your inner journey. Your every thought, word, and deed have a ripple effect. Whether you are near or far from other individuals' consciousness, the ripple effect of your thoughts, words, and deeds may have a positive or negative influence.

When you open your eyes and get up from your cushion, your prayer does not end. The flow of your life should be seamless twenty-four/seven. There is no time when you are other than a spiritual being. The interior freedom to engage (or not) continues in your daily activities.

A pause now and then is expected along the way. Jesus understands, and although at times, the awareness of His presence seems to fade, it is only your awareness that has dulled, *not* Jesus' presence. You are not starting over, beginning again, nor going backward. You are continuing.

Practice is the key. Sit for a few minutes, twice-a-day, and rest in the awareness of your Spiritual Heart Center *area* again and again. Like the prodigal son, you are returning to your Father's house. Jesus awaits your return with patience.

15

Six Additional Mini Meditation Prayer Practices
Staying Grounded

From the Christ Centered Prayer revelation comes six additional prayer practices to help you with the Christ Centered Prayer method and your adjustment to living a balanced life. Jesus gives you the necessary help to move you on your spiritual journey as smoothly as possible. When practiced as needed, these prayer practices may promote stability and balance in your spiritual awakening progress.

1. Power Prayer Meditation

The Power Prayer is a dialog practice that may allow you to address incredibly difficult mental issues that repeatedly arise in your mind states of consciousness. It is its own unique dialog prayer method and is to be used short-term only when necessary. Its sole purpose is to remove invested power in a specific, emotionally charged situation. It does not replace your twice-daily silent Christ Centered Prayer practice. Also, the Power Prayer practice is never to be mixed with your Christ Centered Prayer practice.

Emotional, tormenting rising thoughts are conditioned responses. They may be experienced as a positive or negative solid steel form that seems impenetrable. It is because you have previously given the emotional tormenting rising thoughts power, having accepted a false belief in them, that attempting to make the least dent may be a considerable struggle. However, that which appears as strong as steel may bend to your will and melt in the furnace of your recognition that a conditioned sense-impression has only the power you give it.

When practicing, it is most important to remember the immediacy of responding, "NO POWER, GOD IS." The "NO POWER" is your recognition that the tormenting thought of itself has no power. The "GOD IS" acknowledges that only God is and right there in the moment of the tormenting thought's rising, God alone exists.

The Power Prayer Practice:

- When a tormenting thought rises, silently repeat, "No Power, God Is," as often as is necessary during your daily activities.

- Immediately refocus your attention on the outer activity.

The Power Prayer may bring you into a neutral zone of non-responding and restore your inner peace. Never practice the Power Prayer method while driving or operating any mechanical equipment. Do not practice any prayer method or meditation in your parked car and immediately drive. Always be sure you are fully alert before driving. Whenever your safety is at issue, DO NOT practice any form of prayer method or meditation.

2. Hand-to-Heart Meditation Prayer

The hand-to-heart prayer method is to be practiced in a spiritual energy crisis or at a time of needed guidance. As you practice the Christ Centered Prayer, many inner changes may begin to occur. An expansive consciousness creates times of highs and lows. At times your energy may vibrate so rapidly that you feel as if you are on a roller coaster. You may not understand what is happening, and if immediate help is not available, the silent hand-to-heart prayer may be a short-term solution. This prayer method may be practiced anywhere, in any position, and during any activity that does *not* involve your safety.

The Hand-to-Heart Prayer Practice

- Place your hand over the Spiritual Heart Center area (center of the chest between the breasts).

- Take a long, deep breath, and exhale slowly, relaxing your mind and body. Rest your attention on your hand, not your Spiritual Heart Center, in the silence of awareness. If necessary, repeat several times.

The silent Hand-to-Heart Prayer practice may help bring immediate calm and restore your vibrating energy's balance. Do not let the simplicity of the hand-to-heart prayer practice fool you. Many times, Jesus used His hands to heal, bless, or still the waters. The Holy Spirit, in the name of Jesus Christ, empowers the Hand-to-Heart Prayer.

3. The Listening-In Meditation Prayer

The Christ Centered Prayer is continually guiding you within to your Spiritual Heart Center. The listening-in prayer method may allow you to come to hear the silent, sacred language of God that you may come to understand more easily than any language of this world. *"It is the spirit that quickeneth; the flesh profiteth nothing: the words that I speak unto you, they are spirit, and they are life"* (John 6:63).

The Listening-In Prayer Practice
- Sit, take a long deep breath, slowly exhale, and relax. Turn your hearing inward toward the awareness of your Spiritual Heart Center area (center of the chest, between the breasts).

- Softly listen-in as though you were waiting for a phone to ring.

- Listen to the silence. Be patient and quiet for a few minutes. Then go about your outer business.

The silent space you visit in awareness reveals whatever it is you need at the moment. The listening-in prayer is a separate silent prayer practice. It is not to be mixed with your Christ Centered Prayer practice. The Listening-In prayer may also benefit and improve relationships with family and friends. During a listening-in prayer practice, your silent inner hearing may deepen. You may find clarity of perception in the discernment of conflicting points of view. Discernment arises with compassion and brings a quick resolution to a present moment's need. Discernment thrives in a listening-in environment.

While listening-in to the inner silence within your Spiritual Heart Center, you may find there is a silent, sacred language that speaks to you. The silent voice of God may arise. *"The tongue of the wise useth knowledge aright: but the mouth of fools poureth out foolishness"* (Prov. 15:2).

In the silence of your Spiritual Heart Center, there is an openness rooted in the bedrock of God's abiding presence. As you practice the listening-in prayer, the inner silence deepens. Answers to the questions or the solutions you seek may manifest through individuals, situations, objects, or whatever is necessary. The Holy Spirit, in the name of Jesus, is always communicating with you. Listen-in, and you may hear. *"Who hath ears to hear, let him hear"* (Matt. 13:9).

4. The Temptation Meditation Prayer

The Temptation Meditation Prayer is a silent, mental sword that gives you the power to cut to the quick temptations in their conceptual stage. Temptations want what you have (a realized consciousness). If given the opportunity, they will trample all over your insights, revelations, and realizations. When you are comfortable with your spiritual progress, temptations may arise and come at you in the fiercest ways possible.

The further along you are on your spiritual journey, the more intense temptations become. And they never cease. They will use any means and seem to have a life of their own. After God had affirmed that Jesus was His beloved Son, Jesus was tempted in the wilderness. *"Than was Jesus led up of the Spirit into the wilderness to be tempted of the devil"* (Matt. 4:1).

Temptations never desist. Right up to your passing, a temptation will rise to play with your mind. *"And at the ninth hour, Jesus cried with a loud voice, saying, El-o-i, El-o-i, la-ma sa-bach tha-ni? Being interpreted, "My God, my God, why hast thou forsaken me?"* (Mark 15:34).

Temptations are seducers that invite you to betray the Christ of your being. Strive to be more like the seed that fell upon the good ground. *"But that on the good ground are they, which in an honest and good heart, having heard the word, keep it, and bring forth fruit with patience"* (Luke 8:15).

Once grounded in truth, you have the upper hand. You have the strength not only to refuse a temptation's offer but to grow stronger in conscious awareness of temptations. Scripture offers guidance that may provide armor against the arrows of the tempter in all its disguises. It does not matter if a temptation appears as a person, situation, friend, or foe. The temptation prayer practice is the same. Stay alert to the possibilities of a rising temptation.

The Temptation Prayer Practice
- When temptation rises, mentally, silently say, "Get thee behind me, Satan."

- Silently, mentally repeat the phrase as often as the temptation rises. Do not dialogue or mentally engage with the rising temptation. A temptation thrives on chatter.

Being a disciple of Jesus Christ is an invitation for temptations to rise. The more you resist, the stronger and more persistent temptations become. They feed on your strength. Do not be fooled by what temptations may present. They may come to you with very appealing offers. It is the work of a temptation to make you an offer difficult to overcome.

5. Healing Prayer Meditation

Many well-known shrines worldwide (France, Portugal, and Mexico City are a few) are dedicated to the Blessed Mother Mary. Many individuals have visited these shrines. Many have found the guidance, comfort, healing, and peace they sought. Blessed Mother Mary is a guide *and* a healer. When there is a physical or emotional need, Blessed Mother Mary's healing prayer may heal and comfort.

Healing Prayer Practice

- Lie down on your back and close your eyes. Place one hand on your Spiritual Heart Center area (chest, between the breasts) and your other hand on your abdomen.

- Take a long, deep inhalation breath and slowly exhale. Relax your entire body and mind. Let go of all thoughts, plans, and expectations.

- Slowly and contemplatively listen to every word as you say three Hail Mary's and one Glory Be.

- Rest and trust in knowing that you are in the arms of Mother Mary. She may heal and comfort a broken heart or a broken body.

You may rise from your rest whenever you wish. Rise slowly and allow yourself to become fully alert before moving around. There is no required time. Relax, let go, and trust Mother Mary. These are the only requirements.

You may receive the opposite of that which is expected. Your life may have secret places that are more broken than the obvious. Healing and comfort may not always manifest as you wish. You may have times when emotional healing is more necessary for your life than a physical one. You must trust Mother Mary. As it is with Jesus, Mother Mary's guidance is always in your welfare's best interest.

6. Scripture Meditation Prayer

The scriptures hold within each word the sacredness of your journey. The scripture prayer is a practice of praying the Christian scriptures. The Christian scriptures contain the entire spiritual journey that leads to the Oneness of awareness of your spirituality and the detachments.

The scriptures walk with you every step of the way from Genesis to Revelations. The Christian scriptures (New Testament) are the teachings of Jesus Christ. The scriptures are multileveled. They express themselves at a literal, metaphysical, and mystical level. You are reading your different states of consciousness.

There are many states, frequencies of individual expressions of consciousness. Each individual expression of consciousness brings the consciousness level to the scriptures that enables it to receive at its level of need. Form the habit of listening-in to whatever scripture you have chosen. As your consciousness changes, so may the translations of the scriptures.

The Scripture Prayer Practice

- Choose any scripture word, sentence, or verse. Read slowly and contemplatively.

- Bring your attention to your Spiritual Heart Center area and softly, quietly listen-in to the silence.

- Sit and allow whatever you are seeking to understand to rise. Allow the thoughts of Jesus' teaching to rise, and the mind will translate.

The Scripture Prayer Practice is active because you are actively listening-in. It is beneficial in opening up the depth and breadth of Holy Scripture to your conscious awareness. Do not drift into the rising thoughts of the mind. Be patient. You cannot rush the practice.

Pray the Scriptures a few minutes as often as you like. Do not attempt to figure out mentally the scripture's meaning. Always return to your Spiritual Heart Center area and again listen-in to the silence.

Praying the Christian scriptures may enhance your Christ Centered Prayer practice and progress you on your spiritual journey. The Scripture Prayer practice may prepare you to receive scripture revelations. When you are ready, nothing in the scriptures will be denied.

~~

You have been gifted with six additional helpful prayer practices. Use them in gratitude as often as necessary. They may serve you well.

SUMMARY

The detachment realizations give freedom from attachments and suffering, allowing relationships and using the things in this world to be enjoyed without suffering. Detachments are occurring during The Christ Centered Prayer practice. Detachments may gradually occur. They are *subtle*. A meditation practice may help prepare and ready you.

When you live out of any detachment realization, you continue to experience rising thoughts and emotions. The change is that you are no longer attached to them. You come to live out from a more profound compassionate nature that is unconditional loving for yourself and all individual consciousness expressions.

Detachments require patience and understand*ing and* a sense of humor. Living in a calm state of being is not numbness. It is living as an aware, conscious being.

Any additional Mini Meditations or a review of the obstacles may progress your Christ Centered Meditation and guide you more easily through detachments. Your inner journey is a challenging one, but it is the most rewarding one. Detachment freedom may be yours for the practice. Begin yours now!

~~

*You are Heaven and
Earth
and all things in
between.
You are a Moment now
seen and unseen.*

crm

~~

Author

Carla R. Mancari is a prolific author, life guide and teacher. She leads retreats to improve individuals' (from all walks of life) self-confidence and self-esteem; and enable them to meet life's challenges. For more than 45 years, she has guided individuals in understanding life's spiritual principles, spiritual activities, and rising emotions in their private and daily lives. Her greatest joy is helping individuals to realize their self-worth, unique gifts/talents, full potential, *and* to wake-up to their spirituality.

Carla is the recipient of The Christ Centered Prayer revelation, The Minute Method, and The Heart-Centered Practice. She is a co-founder of the Contemplative Invitation Teaching. Although Carla had never attended high school and was labeled a retarded child, she attained two University degrees: a B.A. from the University of South Carolina in Columbia, South Carolina, and an MEd from South Carolina State University in Orangeburg, South Carolina. Carla studied at Brigham Young University and attended the School of the Americas in Switzerland.

Carla led a class-action suit in the United States Supreme Court for the protection of minorities' rights (Morton vs. Mancari, 1973) and was a certified psychologist. She served in the United States Air Force. Traveling worldwide for many years, Carla studied with Christian, Hindu, and Buddhist masters. She was a guest on the Larry King Show, guest lecturer at various colleges, professional groups, and book signings.

Carla gained national recognition when featured in *Good Housekeeping*, "The Education of Carla Mancari, 1969." It chronicled her life in 1967-68 when she was the first white student to receive a Master's degree from the then all-Black South Carolina State College in Orangeburg, South Carolina.

Websites:
www.TheMinuteMethodPractice.com
www.ChristCenteredPrayerPractice.com

Author's Books

Casey-Martus, Sandra, and Mancari, Carla R. *The Lessons Volume One*: *How to Understand Spiritual Principles, Spiritual Activities, and Rising Emotions.* Previously 2008, Recently 2017, Celestial Literary Group.

- - - *The Lessons Volume Two*: *How to Understand Spiritual Principles, Spiritual Activities, and Rising Emotions.* Celestial Literary Group, 2017.

- - - *The Lessons Volume Three*: *How to Understand Spiritual Principles, Spiritual Activities, and Rising Emotions.* Celestial Literary Group, 2017.

- - - *The Lessons Volume Four*: *How to Understand Spiritual Principles, Spiritual Activities, and Rising Emo-*

tions. Celestial Literary Group, 2017.

- - - *The Christ Centered Prayer: Revelation, Strait Gate and Narrow Way.* Celestial Literary Group, 2018

- - - *Your Other Heart: The Best Kept Secret.* Celestial Literary Group, 2011.

- - - *The Scripture Prayer: Praying The Scriptures.* Celestial Literary Group, 2020.

Carpenter, Mary B., and Mancari, Carla R. *A Scriptural Reference: For The Lessons: How to Understand Spiritual Principles, Spiritual Activities, and Rising Emotions, Volumes 1-4.* Celestial Literary Group, 2019.

Mancari, Carla R., *When Jesus Is the Guru: A Wayward Christian's Spiritual Walk.* Celestial Literary Group, 2010.

\- - - *Eco-You, A Power of One, Improve Your Health, Improve Your Life.* Previously published Bloomington, IN, WestBow Press, 2011. Celestial Literary Group, 2019.

\- - - *A Diet for the Soul: The Minute Method.* Previously published Bloomington, IN, WestBow Press, 2011. Celestial Literary Group, 2019.

\- - - *Walking on the Grass: A White Woman In A Black World.* Previously published Mercer Press, 2002. Celestial Literary Group, 2016.

\- - - *The Minute Method* Book 1*: It's Life Changing! Realize Your Full Potential,*. Previously published Wheatmark, 2012. Celestial Literary Group, 2018.

\- - -*The Minute Method Book 2: Workbook – Companion to The Minute Method Book 1: It's Life Changing*

– *Realize Your Full Potential*. The Celestial Literary Group, 2017.

- - - *The Minute Method Book3: The Essentials –Quick Study Guide.* Celestial Literary Group, 2017.

- - - *The Minute Method Book 4: At The Foot of The Guru: Stories*. Celestial Literary Group, 2017.

- - - *The Minute Method Book 5: The Three of You, You Are Never Alone*. Celestial Literary Group, 2017.

- - - *The 4th Chakra: Your Spiritual Heart Center – How to Quickly Access It*. Celestial Literary Group, 2016.

- - - *Abortion and The Bible: The Abortion Dilemma: A Scriptural Response, A Woman's Spirituality.* Celestial Literary Group, 2017.

- - - *Racism: The Pain of Invisibility.* Celestial Literary Group, 2017.

- - - *The Rising Emotions: Understanding and Mastering Them.* Celestial Literary Group, 2017.

- - - *The Mystical Path: The Serious Student.* Celestial Literary Group, 2017.

- - - *Spiritual Principles: Understanding, Realizing, and Living Them.* Celestial Literary Group, 2018.

- - *Climate Change: Consciousness Change.* Celestial Literary Group, 2017.

- - - *Words: Locks On The Door or Keys To The Kingdom.* Celestial Literary Group, 2018.

- - - *Aging: Physical to the Mystical.* Celestial Literary Group, 2018.

- - - *Divine Love: Your Nature.* Celestial Literary Group, 2018.

- - - *The Lazarus Rising: The Kundalini – A Rising Dormant Energy.* Celestial Literary Group, 2018.

- - - *Depression: Hopelessness.* Celestial Literary Group, 2018.

- - - *Jesus Christ: Teacher.* Celestial Literary Group, 2018.

- - - *The Transformation: Change of Heart.* Celestial Literary Group, 2018.

- - - *The Mystical Surrender: Giving In.* Celestial Literary Group, 2018.

- - - *Death Ain't Dead: Empty Graves.* Celestial Literary Group, 2018.

- - - *Common Decency: Your DNA.* Celestial Literary Group, 2018.

- - - *Christians: Common Decency.* Celestial Literary Group, 2018.

- - - *Beyond Buddhism: Meditations.* Celestial Literary Group, 2018.

- - - *Exit: Get Ready, Set, Go.* Celestial Literary Group, 2018.

- - - *Meditation: Good For You.* Celestial Literary Group, 2018.

- - - *How To Love "You" - Begin with You.* Celestial Literary Group, 2018.

- - - *Consciousness: Yours.* Celestial Literary Group, 2018.

- - - *Suicide: Understanding It.* Celestial Literary Group, 2018.

- - - *Detachment: Realizations.* Celestial Literary Group, 2018.

- - - *Sexual Abuse: By The Church – Its Root, Coerced Celibacy.* Celestial Literary Group, 2018.

- - - *Guns and Guts: The Courage To Act.* Celestial Literary Group, 2018.

\- - - *Book of Prayerful Christian Meditations.* Celestial Literary Group, 2018.

\- - - *Jesus, The Way: A Mystical Understanding.* Celestial Literary Group, 2019.

\- - - *Motivation: Self-Motivated.* Celestial Literary Group, 2019.

\- - - *Totally Free: Is Killing Me.* Celestial Literary, Group, 2018.

\- - - *A Thirty Second Meditation For Teenagers.* Celestial Literary Group, 2018.

\- - - *A Thirty Second Meditation For Seniors.* Celestial Literary Group, 2017.

\- - - *The Five Faces Of Love. Celestial Literary Group, 2019.*

\- - - *Angel In The House,* Celestial Literary Group, 2019 (A Children's book).

- - - *Put It In The Bible: Prayerful Request,* Celestial Literary Group, 2019.

- - - *Loneliness: Heartache,* Celestial Literary Group, 2019.

- - - *Hate: A Dark Emotion,* Celestial Literary Group, 2019

- - - *Greed: It's Addictive.* Celestial Literary Group, 2019.

- - - *On Being Young: Choices.* Celestial Literary Group, 2019.

- - - *Gratitude: Expressed, Sincere.* Celestial Literary Group, 2019.

- - - *Humor: A Necessity.* Celestial Literary Group, 2019.

- - - *A Christian: Are You One?* Celestial Literary Group, 2019.

- - - *A Habit: How To Switch Meditation Practices.* Celestial Literary Group, 2019.

- - - *Impeachment: Living On The Dark Side.* Celestial Literary Group, 2019.

- - - *The Jesus I Know.* Celestial Literary Group, 2019.

- - - *Grace: Spirit And Truth.* Celestial Literary Group, 2019.

- - - *Temptation.* Celestial Literary Group, 2019.

- - - *The Christian Journey – Teacher Student Relationship.* Celestial Literary Group, 2019.

- - - *The Beloved - Who Is The Beloved?* Celestial Literary Group, 2019.

- - - *What If I Were Gay?* Celestial Literary Group, 2019.

- - - *Mother Mary – Mother of Jesus.* Celestial Literary Group, 2019.

- - - *I Remember America.* Celestial Literary Group, 2019.

- - - *The Overcoming - "Jesus."* Celestial Literary Group, 2019.

- - - *When Faith Is Not Enough.* Celestial Literary Group, 2019.

- - - *The Plane of Opposites: The Work.* Celestial Literary Group, 2020.

- - - *The Heart-Centered Practice: Revelation.* Celestial Literary Group, 2020.

- - - *Crisis.* Celestial Literary Group, 2020.

- - - *Grief: Gut-Wrenching Emotion.* Celestial Literary Group, 2020.

- - - *God.* Celestial Literary Group, 2020.

---. *Regrets: Do You Have Any?* Celestial Literary Group, 2020.

---. *1968, 1968,1968: The Mind of A Racist.* Celestial Literary Group, 2020.

---. *Satan.* Celestial Literary Group, 2020.

---. *Spirituality: Yours.* Celestial Literary Group, 2020.

NOTES

Made in the USA
Coppell, TX
07 March 2021